Rat and Cat

in

The Dance

Written by
Jeanne Willis

Illustrated by
Gabriele Antonini

Rat was looking at a book.

"Got you Rat!" said Cat.
"Let me go!" said Rat.

"I will do a cool thing," said Rat.
"Will you?" said Cat.

"I will do a cool dance,"
said Rat.

"This will be my dress," said Rat.

"This will be my wig," said Rat.

"Dress up, then!" said Cat.

Rat hid.
"No peeking Cat!" he said.

"Look!" said Rat.
He did his cool dance.

"Eek!" said Cat.
"I can see Rat's pants!"
Rat ran off.

"I will get you Rat!" said Cat.